Merna

Happy Birthday

1984

God's love and ours:

Herb, Ruth and
family

garden meditations

garden meditations

Josephine Robertson

Illustrations by Billie Jean Osborne

Abingdon
NASHVILLE

GARDEN MEDITATIONS

Copyright © 1977 by Abingdon

Library of Congress Cataloging in Publication Data

ROBERTSON, JOSEPHINE. Garden meditations. 1. Nature (Theology)—Meditations. 2. Gardening—Meditations. I. Title.
BT695.5.R62   242'.4   77-23316

ISBN 0-687-14000-5

MANUFACTURED BY THE PARTHENON PRESS AT NASHVILLE, TENNESSEE, UNITED STATES OF AMERICA

Dedicated to My Friends
at
the Denver Botanic Gardens

contents

For Joy in God's Creation

O Heavenly Father, who hast filled the world with beauty; Open, we beseech thee, our eyes to behold thy gracious hand in all thy works; that rejoicing in thy whole creation, we may learn to serve thee with gladness.

Book of Common Prayer 1928

bruised herbs

The heavier cross, the heartier prayer;
The bruised herbs most fragrant are. . . .
And David's psalms had ne'er been sung
If grief his heart had never wrung.
Benjamin Schmolke

The first snow of winter fell wet and thick, but the temperature had not dropped far below freezing. I went out to the garden with a broom to sweep aside the cover from the chrysanthemums, hoping to find enough undamaged to fill a large vase. Sure enough, when I snapped their long stems and shook their snowy heads, they were fresh as ever. The annuals had not fared so well. Petunias and zinnias were wilted beyond repair, but as I pushed the snow aside, up came a strong scent from the broken stems of wet marigolds. This was not the sweet perfume of petunia or alyssum, but an earthy pungence that seemed to say, "Summer is over."

How many associations we have with "bruised" stems! The fragrance of fresh-cut grass, the sweet smell of new-mown hay, the tempting whiff of

marigolds

plucked mint—and one that is lost to most of us—the incense of burning leaves. As children, we jumped into the crisp piles, watched fascinated as our fathers touched a match, and gazed intently as smoke curled toward an autumn sky, giving off an aroma forever associated with blue skies, scudding clouds, apples, and pumpkins.(Though better for the atmosphere, today's plastic bags and compost piles seem drab endings for autumn's glory.) We enjoy, too, the fragrance of rose and lavender stripped from their stems and dried for the days when winter has killed the blooms.

The little-known poet who wrote the lines above knew his garden plants and his fellowman. Sometimes bitter disappointments can result in unforeseen good. From suffering we can learn compassion, and from overcoming obstacles, with God's help, we can grow in strength and courage. From bruised herbs comes a special fragrance.

Help us, we pray, to distill wisdom from experience and, with this deeper understanding, to help others.

a garden is a poem

If thou draw out thy soul to the hungry, and satisfy the afflicted soul; . . . thou shalt be like a watered garden.

Isaiah 58:10-11

One of the charms of gardening is that the gardener can make his own rules as he goes along. If he thinks squash goes well with lemon lilies, he is free to mix them. No two gardens are alike because they are expressions of personality. Each is an individual creation, as is a poem. We know that some poems turn out better than others, but surely not because they follow any set form. A poem, like a garden, is unique.

The vegetable grower is a practical person. Fresh corn, sun-sweetened tomatoes, and tender peas are his kind of poetry, which has an easy rhythm. The rock garden of a scientist, with each plant flourishing in a discrete niche, has an intricate meter. The garden of a person too busy or forgetful to weed and water is like a verse that doesn't rhyme very well. The well-organized person who sticks to a long-range plan of adding tulips here, roses there, has a meter correct and precise. The experimenter who tries anything new, who brings in roadside specimens or nonconforming transplants from a neighbor's garden, enjoys just as much satisfaction from his efforts as the others, even if the result is very free verse.

Our gardens suggest something about our personalities, and personalities are what other people encounter. Those with whom we come in contact form certain impressions based on the attitudes they find, whether casual, careful, happy, or melancholy. We build these patterns through our everyday thinking and activities.

To be sure, there are factors in our lives truly beyond our control—just as hail or grasshoppers may ravage our plantings. Physical handicaps may be limiting; poverty may plague us; loving relationships may falter; grief may shake our foundations. And yet, an invalid may take a lively interest in the world outside and send his callers away refreshed. A person who has known grief and disappointment may transcend his private sorrows by focusing his interest on the future and on the concerns of others.

The patient cultivation of faith, concern, and optimism can create gardens of tranquility. Here friend and stranger may find the poetry of joy and compassion.

Help us to cultivate in our lives the things that are good, pure, and beautiful, that they may flower for the joy of others.

chancel flowers

Give unto the Lord the glory due unto his name:
bring an offering, and come before him: worship the
Lord in the beauty of holiness.

I Chronicles 16:29

Members of the congregation who view the
flowers in the chancel on a Sunday morning may
enjoy the splash of color against a somber
background, but their reactions seldom go beyond
"Very nice" or "Could be better," as they turn
their attention to loftier matters. The arranger,
however, particularly if a novice, sits in their midst
thinking, "Why didn't I bring that branch over
farther? There isn't enough foliage—the yellow
lilies are fading into the wall. The spray is
drooping."

Few situations in life give us such an opportunity
to contemplate our mistakes, but no opportunity to
rectify them. Probably only we who have tried our
hand at this know how much love and planning go
into the chancel flowers. Usually we begin thinking
about the possibilities early in the week, keeping an
eye (unless in the heart of the city) on our own

17

garden, our neighbor's, and the roadside wild flowers. Experience brings confidence and speed, but as beginners we are uneasy, knowing that a church full of people will be gazing at our creation. We want it to be beautiful, even if we know it will never be mistaken for the work of a professional florist. We watch the work of the experts and are surprised at some of the materials they find effective: branches of apple blossoms in the spring, showy sunflowers that border backroads from midsummer to frost, branches of scarlet crab apples, and, in the fall, teasels, dried yucca, or staghorn sumac combined with chrysanthemums.

We learn to plan ahead. One plants zinnias, another gladioli, thinking them just the right size and color to use against the background. Another, an expert with geraniums, gladdens our hearts on the first Sunday of January with a cluster of pots holding bright red blooms to salute the new season of growth.

We learn, too, to back off and take a long look at the work of our hands. Sometimes an arrangement that looks much too large close up proves to be just right from the back of the church. We treasure the experience of working with flowers in the quiet of the sanctuary, with light streaming through the windows, perhaps some music from the organ, and a feeling of hushed expectancy.

In due course, as we learn from our mistakes, we develop confidence. Even if we still see points for improvement, we can view our creation with equanimity and, along with the other worshipers, turn our thoughts to loftier matters.

Bless the efforts of those who work, however humbly, to beautify thy house of worship.

partnerships

Blest be the tie that binds
Our hearts in Christian love,
The fellowship of kindred minds
Is like to that above.

John Fawcett

One of the most amazing partnerships in nature is responsible for the lichen. We see the rough cover of lichens on rock—gray, brownish, black, yellow, gray-green, and sometimes orange in color. They grow in a tight mat and consist of a combination of algae and fungi. Each is necessary to the other, and through their chemical reaction occurs a slow disintegration of rock into soil that makes later plant life possible. The alga, a green plant, lives with the fungus in a manner known as symbiotic, defined as "the consorting together, usually in mutually advantageous partnership, of dissimilar organisms." The term is from the Greek, meaning "living together" or "companionship." These "pioneer plants" through the centuries create thin layers of soil where mosses, grasses, plants, then trees may grow.

This "mutually advantageous partnership" makes us think of other partnerships. Business and professional collaboration can often accomplish more than individual effort. Doctors can serve better through group practices. Ministers benefit from the special skills of their associates. Today's scientific research is usually pursued by teams. But perhaps the closest analogy to a partnership is that of a good marriage.

In a successful marriage each partner makes an unique and essential contribution to the intimate relationship. Together, the partners find mutual support, happy companionship, comfort, encouragement, shared adventures and sorrows, and the miracle of the loved and welcomed child. At a time when traditional bonds are challenged, those who have known truly good marriages can attest that here they have found their deepest human happiness.

When a human life is God-inspired, this too is a partnership; for God gives strength, and the individual can further the divine purposes. Certain men and women have a radiance that shows this inspiration. The lichen on the rock is a humble example, but in its own way it is the perfect symbol of fruitful partnership.

Our Father, we thank thee for close ties, human and divine, and pray that these ties may be rich and productive.

eyes to see,
hearts to care

The God of seasons; whose pervading power
Controls the sun or sheds his fleecy shower:
He bids each flower His quickening word obey,
Or to each lingering bloom enjoins delay.

Gilbert White

One need not travel far to find adventure in the world of nature. Two hundred years ago a curate in an English village began keeping notes on the birds, the plants, the seasons, and wildlife and sending them in letters full of wonder and discovery to a like-minded friend. Before his death in 1793 he condensed his knowledge into a small volume entitled *The Natural History of Selborne*. This unpretentious work has gone through one hundred fifty printings and is so beloved by its readers that Selborne has become almost a mecca for naturalists, a circumstance beyond the dreams of modest Gilbert White.

Our own town, at the foot of the mountains, is laced with irrigation ditches that, during the growing season, rush water from mountain streams to sunbaked farms on the plains. For much of the year they stand empty, brown and dry. Few notice them then, except small boys searching for ''found'' objects. However, when a shortage of funds curtailed field trips by bus from our schools, a gifted teacher of natural science was not dismayed. ''We don't have to travel to see exciting things,'' he asserted. ''Let's explore the ditch in back of the school.''

He began taking groups of children to see what they could find, encouraging them to look closely and to ask questions. They found seeds—seeds of plums, apples, chokecherries, box elder, cotton-wood, and the hips of wild roses. They brought the seeds back to their classrooms to explore through the eye of the microscope, and then planted some themselves. How strange that the shrubby chokecherry had a larger seed than the towering cottonwood! They saw how small trees leaned to the east, and became curious about prevailing winds and compasses. They poked in fallen leaves decaying in puddles and realized, for the first time, that leaf mold can help things grow. There seemed to be no life in the ditch, until a log, turned over, revealed a lively colony of spiders.

One lucky boy picked up a stone that fell apart and revealed the clear imprint of a leaf. From that moment the fossil search was on. The children could have read about these things in textbooks, but how much more exciting to have the experience of discovery!

In the world of people there is even more to discover. As we speed to our activities by car, we no longer have the opportunity for leisurely chats across hedges or encounters with fellow walkers; but wherever we meet with people, there are discoveries awaiting—if we only care.

Help us to realize that just as those with eyes to see can find adventure in everyday surroundings, so those with hearts to care can find unsuspected depths in persons they come to know.

ϝriendship corner

Believeth all things, hopeth all things, endureth all things.

I Corinthians 13:7

She was a nurse who lived alone in part of an old house in a downtown area. Until she moved there—to be near the hospital where she worked—she had always had a garden. Those who love gardening know that the urge can stay strong, especially in spring when markets offer their tempting flats of little plants. The only unpaved area nearby was the corner where two sidewalks intersected, leaving a six-foot square of hard-packed dirt. What would people think, she wondered, if she planted some flowers there? Surely there was no law against it.

There were curious glances when she went to work, digging up the hard soil, fertilizing, planting, setting out seedlings; but the sunshine and watering produced a colorful mass of bloom. Each spring she added new things—tomatoes, roses, herbs, Shasta daisies—all crowded together and apparently quite happy that way.

27

There were other results. As she spent her free hours working on the little garden, she was surprised to find how interested people were: pedestrians on their way to work, elderly people on their way to market, youngsters going to school, pet owners on their daily rounds. So many people stopped to chat that she called her garden "Friendship Corner." A Boy Scout told her it was the most beautiful garden in town, and she glimpsed long-haired young people down on their patched knees smelling the roses.

Then, one morning, she went out and found that the daisies had all been cut. A few days later, the roses had been broken off with long stems, which meant it would take weeks for new buds to form. It was hard to believe there were vandals on Friendship Corner! As she loosened the soil on that discouraging morning, one of her regulars went past, an elderly merchant who had come to this country and worked hard to make a new start. She told him what had happened and wondered aloud if there was any use in going on.

"Keep right on," he told her. "You are doing a good and beautiful thing. Don't let the bad ones win!"

This was just the advice she needed. Soon she

was putting hand-lettered signs among the flowers, such as:

"God made me a pretty white daisy. I'm happy in my little spot under the Colorado sky, nodding at the passersby. Please don't carry me off!"

The signs began to attract as much interest as the flowers, and the vandalism, perhaps by coincidence, stopped. The "bad ones" did not win, and the flowers, unprotected by wall or fence, continued to bring pleasure to many. The gardener long remembered those words of encouragement. "You are doing a good and beautiful thing. Keep on."

When discouragement strikes hard, grant us the faith to overcome setbacks and to continue our work with love.

tReasure

Feed my sheep.
John 21:17

On the campus of Colorado State University at Fort Collins stands a handsome stone building bearing the name National Seed Storage Laboratory, USDA. It is unique in our country and the first of its kind in the world. We have all heard of the gold treasured at Fort Knox. This holds a different kind of treasure.

Within its walls are storage rooms with thousands of shiny pint cans, each containing seeds of grains, vegetables, trees, or flowers. Many of these seeds come from remote parts of the world and represent the original, primitive strains from which plantsmen have developed new varieties. But sometimes the hybrids, which at first seem to be miraculous improvements, begin to show susceptibility to rust, blight, or insect attack. However, if the primitive seed is still available, the hybridist can go back, start over, and develop a variety designed to resist such ravages. The seeds in the shiny cans are checked at regular intervals for viability, and if stock becomes low, some are planted in a favorable climate to build up the supply.

At a time when hunger looms as a world problem, the United Nations has recognized the importance of seed banks, and through its Food and Agricultural Organization (FAO), it has advocated setting up a global chain of such facilities. Many of the seeds were obtained with great effort by adventurous collectors. When the sturdy, primitive strains are lost, it becomes increasingly difficult to replace them, since their sources in the wilds of even remote countries are becoming populated and in many cases closed to foreigners.

As one walks through the laboratories where botanists are doing their research, and on into the cool, quiet rooms where thousands of cans carrying the potential for fields of grain are stored, one senses the presence of wonderful riches.

Sometimes it is important to go back to our own spiritual sources, to get away from today's complexities and turn to the simple truths, preserved at great cost by ancient Jews and early Christians. In our sacred writings there is a seed bank of inspiration. Fortunately for those of us who are not theologians, we can lay aside volumes of disputation and exposition and return to the seminal teachings—Love God, love thy neighbor.

Lead us, we pray, to a new stewardship of earth's life-giving grains, whereby in the name of Christ, who was unwilling to send the multitude away hungry, nations may work together to banish forever the specter of hunger.

flowers to help
a hospital

To rejoice in his labor; this is the gift of God.

Ecclesiastes 5:19

In the lobby of a local hospital, for the past several years, a flower stand displaying pots of violets, gloxinias, and trailing vines growing under lights has attracted thousands of visitors. A small sign above the entrancing rainbow of colors explains that the profits go to the hospital. What the sign does not say is that these flowers have been the special project of a woman, now in her seventies, who has turned her hobby into heart monitors, crash carts, and circoelectric beds. Her dream is that the funds, totaling several thousand dollars in the past ten years, will help make possible a therapeutic bathing pool.

Growing houseplants had not been a lifetime hobby for her; it began after she saw the results of her grown son's experiments with plant growing. On one occasion he had asked to use his parents'

33

house, which had a humidifier, to start off some plants under lights. After she saw how the seedlings flourished, she tried some violet cuttings and gloxinia seeds and was delighted with her own results. When she noticed that occasional potted plants sold quickly at the hospital gift shop, she began taking her surplus there. From this began a major activity. Her husband put in more lights, built shelves in the kitchen, dining, and living rooms, and even the guest room, until the house was almost a conservatory. Together they transported cartons of plants in white plastic pots to the gift shop and brought back florists' containers left behind when patients went home. These were transformed into attractive planters with assorted foliage.

Not all the plants went to hospital rooms. Many were purchased by visitors and doctors for home enjoyment. From these sales the grower took only enough to cover expenses.

My friend has been active in many social and church concerns, but when advancing years and the loss of her husband necessitated cutting back on them, the flower project was the last to go. This was the one closest to her heart. It involved hard work, but there was special pleasure in knowing not only that she was helping, but that others enjoyed the flowers that had been her own joy.

Each of us has some special ability—even a modest one—and there is a special satisfaction in using it for others.

Grant that we may find ways to use whatever talents or abilities we have in joyful service to others.

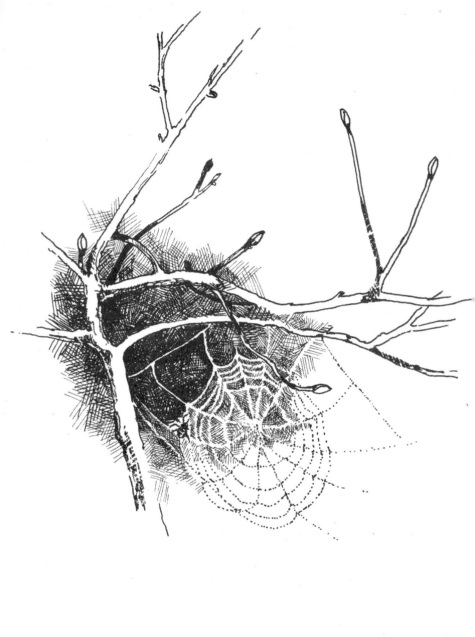

gardens of trees

I will put in the wilderness the cedar, the acacia, the myrtle, and the olive; I will set in the desert the cypress, the plane and the pine together; that men may see and know, may consider and understand together, that the hand of the Lord has done this.

Isaiah 41:19-20 RSV

While most people have a general idea of what an arboretum is—something like a collection of trees—they don't find the idea very exciting, and relatively few people ever visit one. My husband is a tree hobbyist, and wherever we travel, we consult our assorted directories to see which arboreta we can stop at along our way.

Although lacking in the colorful appeal of flowers, as well as in tourist amenities, the gardens of trees have a quiet, impressive spell of their own. The trails are never crowded—unless there is a blossom display in spring or a blaze of color in the fall. There may be a few workmen pruning or raking, a few visitors gazing upward with reference book in hand, or—occasionally—a class of children or Scouts that goes chattering past like a flock of birds; but mostly, there is that special quiet.

The scientific visitor may be delighted to see his first Davidia in bloom, an unusual buckthorn or Evodia, but the nonscientific can find delight in the leafy walks, the interesting signs, the human interest in the arboretum's founding. No two arboreta are alike. One was established, not in Isaiah's "wilderness," but in a city dump; another, on reclaimed sand dunes. One was started by a farmer, who spent his hard-earned money to import exotic species. One was a family project, its founders buried in a peaceful corner; one still has the marble statues and balustrades of a great estate; one has trees planted by famous men; one has a trail marked with bluebird nesting boxes; and one has a great slope farmed long ago and then left fallow, where an enchanting woodland of dogwood has grown up of its own accord.

The great old trees are awesome; it is no wonder they were venerated by primitive man. No longer do we believe that special gods inhabit them. "But if I were a pagan," Paul Tillich, the twentieth-century theologian, told his students, "I would be a tree worshiper."

Each arboretum was established by someone

who loved trees, and since it takes many years for trees to reach maturity, it is often our privilege to see what the founder could only envision. The saplings were planted with faith and hope, and today, they are ours to enjoy. We look at the majesty of mature groves, quiet except for wind in the leaves, birdcall, or scolding squirrel, and agree with Isaiah that "the hand of the Lord has done this."

We thank thee for the beauty and symbolism of trees and pray that our lives may be as those planted by rivers of water that bring forth fruit in their season.

flowering fountains

Ho, everyone that thirsteth, come ye to the waters.

Isaiah 55:1

"Blessed are the merciful." From early childhood I knew what this verse meant, for I had *seen* it. At the low point of the road, between two hills, stood a massive stone fountain with twin streams of water splashing into the smooth, brown basin. While a child perched on the stone base could drink from the spouting streams, the real patrons of the fountain were the horses. They plunged their soft muzzles into the water eagerly, tossing their heads occasionally, until the driver yanked on the reins. Meanwhile water would splash over the rim leaving a polished trail across the deep cut letters, *Blessed are the merciful.*

Wherever an old fountain still stands, it is worth pausing to search for an inscription. On one I found chisled roughly:

Drink of this fountain
Pure and sweet

It flows for rich and poor the same
The cup of water in His name

and on another: "Whosoever will, let him take the water of life freely."

In some places the dry basins have been planted with geraniums, petunias, and trailing vines, bright tributes to the memory of the merciful. The tribute is fitting and well deserved; for these old fountains offered more than water. They were symbols of kindness and compassion. Their donors not only believed the teachings chiseled deep in the stone but put their beliefs into practical form.

Today both horses and foot travelers have all but disappeared. We who hurry down the road by car are not troubled by the thirst felt under a hot sun; nor do we enjoy the wonderful quenching of such thirst by cool spring water. Yet all around us are wayfarers whose spirits seek refreshment. What can we offer them?

As merciful men of an earlier day put thy teaching into practical form, so may we, in our time, find expression for our faith in service.

planting the pits

The wilderness and the solitary place shall be glad for them; and the desert shall rejoice, and blossom as the rose.

Isaiah 35:1

While Archbishop Lamy was working for the completion of his cathedral in the desert town of Santa Fe a century ago, he was also building a garden. Adobe walls enclosed a roomy area behind the cathedral where his own modest house stood. Here he planted shade and fruit trees, cultivated and wild flowers, vegetables, grapevines, and strawberries. In his fine biography *Lamy of Santa Fe* (Farrar, Straus & Giroux, 1975), Paul Horgan tells how the archbishop installed a sparkling fountain, a pool with trout, well-designed paths, and benches where he loved to sit in meditation.

It was a beautiful oasis that amazed and charmed visitors, but it was also a teaching garden. Archbishop Lamy wanted to show what could be done both to improve human diet and to beautify the dusty frontier town. Due to his efforts many trees were planted along the streets. The earliest

42

pictures show a barren cluster of buildings, but those of the 1880s reveal trees all along the streets and in the central plaza.

Obtaining plant materials was no easy matter. With his own money he sent away for fruit and shade trees that had to be freighted across the plains by stagecoach at no small cost. Returning from his own journeys he brought chestnut seeds and saplings in pails of water. His fruits were famous. Sometimes he sold boxes of the prized peaches, grapes, pears, and strawberries, using the money for the support of hospital and orphanage; but much he gave away. When he presented peaches to his friends, he always asked that they plant the pits.

Planting the pits was a homely symbol of his teachings. What his friends enjoyed they were asked to pass along for the benefit of others. Good gifts bear within themselves the seeds of future planting.

One hot summer day when we were moving into a house in a strange town, a neighbor came over with a pitcher of lemonade tinkling with ice. It was too welcome a gesture to be forgotten and has reminded me to do what I can to welcome newcomers. A man helps a student through college. "Don't pay me back," he says. "Help someone else.'' Jesus' teachings were not intended only for the comfort of his listeners; they carried the mandate of sharing with others.

The old archbishop, in asking his friends to plant the pits of his beautiful peaches, had a vision of more orchards in a frontier town; but, in a wordless sermon, he was saying also, ''Don't let your blessings stop with you. Pass them on!''

We thank thee for those who have made the desert places in our own lives and in the world around us to blossom. May we, too, plant seeds that will bring joy to others.

Ready when the moment comes

I never did anything worth doing by accident, nor did any of my inventions come by accident.

Thomas A. Edison

When the drifts begin to melt on Rocky Mountain slopes above timberline, the snow buttercup suddenly dots the rugged field with gold. This lovely flower is a buttercup-in-a-hurry, since its season for blooming and fruiting at an altitude of around ten thousand feet is only a few weeks. The *Ranunculus adoneus* has adapted its way of life in impressive fashion to harsh conditions.

Strong perennial roots reach down under the frosted ground, and buds begin to form early. They can be found under layers of snow long before the shoots can reach the light. Finally a "knuckle" pushes up, and the sun melts little circles around the dark stems. Then suddenly gold chalices an inch across gleam above the damp slopes where the snow is receding. When their chance to break through comes, they are ready. Are we?

snow
buttercups

"What luck!" we may say when an author writes a best seller or an athlete wins a medal, but success has its roots in patient preparation. My friend who writes successful books for children spent many years on little stories, always learning, always ready to tear up the first try and do over the rejected manuscripts. The athlete's trophy crowns long, exhausting practice. A man works at a modest job, giving it the best he has; and when he is promoted, it is not because of luck but because he has proved his ability. The lifeguard, bronzed and handsome, sits on his pedestal seemingly idle. Suddenly he leaps down, plunges into the surf, and rescues a hapless swimmer. He may be a hero, but this is not luck. It is preparation. He is ready when the moment comes.

In our spiritual lives the same principle holds true. If we make Christian love the rule of our lives, it is there when we need reinforcement. It can transform anger into compassion, jealousy into generosity, despair into faith; and it can turn humdrum days into joyous ones. These things do not just happen. Our spiritual roots grow quietly stronger through prayer and practice. When the moment comes for action, we, too, are ready; and our faith can find expression even as the hard-pressed snow buttercup lifts its golden chalice to the sun.

May our long-held thoughts prepare us to respond in thy spirit when the call to action comes.

cottonwood,
friend of the pioneer

Seen across the trackless desert,
Mountain peaks alone with God;
Thank thee Lord for shade and water
In this Chapel Cottonwood.
        Earl Swisher, anniversary hymn

Trees, like fashions, can become very popular and then go out of style. In Victorian days, the *Araucaria araucana,* or monkey-puzzle tree, was a favorite. This evergreen, with bristling, snakelike branches, was planted in front of gingerbread mansions with cupolas, to lend a sinister charm. Specimens are still found on old estates and in arboreta, but not on suburban lawns.

No longer popular, either, for home grounds or parks is the western cottonwood. This is regrettable, since the cottonwood served the pioneers well. As wagon trains lumbered across the plains, travelers watched for a fringe of green in the distance. That meant water and, if the stream were sizable enough, the cooling shade of tall cotton-

49

woods to add to that of alders and willows. How refreshing it was under the shiny, whispering leaves. Such relief from the burning sun!

When homesteaders built their first cabins, they often collected saplings from the creeksides to plant as windbreaks. Today as we drive into the country, we find the homes, built with such effort, dwarfed by their gnarled and towering protectors.

Cottonwoods shielded the lonely homes from wind and sun and furnished wood for fenceposts, fires, and other farm purposes. Children loved to play around their giant roots, to climb on their hospitable limbs, and sometimes, to enjoy the infinite possibilities of a hollow trunk. In spring, small particles from the female trees floated down like gossamer, and masses of white "cotton" created a snow-in-summer effect.

Our own church was founded by a group of pioneers who met to organize in a grove of cottonwoods.

Modern landscapers scorn this tree, claiming the big branches are brittle and the roots soak up too much groundwater. True it is that the unsymmetrical branches reach up in winter like stark, grasping arms, but their distortion speaks of hard and successful battles with the wind.

We have planted a male tree on our side lot where we can watch it grow. We will not see its towering maturity, but birds build nests in its branches, and its shimmering leaves are seldom still.

There is more to a tree—and a person—than symmetry and style. Rugged characters often lack grace; but when they help those in need, they seem beautiful. To us the cottonwood is a symbol of shelter and protection, and we honor it as the friend of the pioneer.

We thank thee for the strong who can offer shelter and refreshment to tired and discouraged travelers along life's way.

meeting
disappointment

For age is opportunity no less
Than youth itself, though in another dress,
And as the evening twilight fades away
The sky is filled with stars, invisible by day.
Henry Wadsworth Longfellow

When early plant-explorers were searching our West for botanical discoveries, the journeys meant packing supplies on mules, traveling by horseback, camping, entering the territory of possibly hostile Indians, and braving rocky trails, desert loneliness, and harsh weather. They sent their specimens back East to experts who had the university libraries and scientific equipment to identify the plants. Best known of these scholars were Dr. John Torrey and his pupil and later colleague, Dr. Asa Gray. Without having set foot in the West themselves, they became authorities on western flora. One of their friends, plant explorer C. C. Parry, named two high peaks near Georgetown, Colorado, in their honor. Both Gray and Torrey longed to see their towering namesakes.

Gray finally made a memorable trip to Georgetown in 1872, when he was sixty-two. With a group of distinguished botanists and local citizens, he climbed to the summit, where, with appropriate ceremonies, the peak was dedicated in his honor. Torrey, seventy-six at the time, longed to be with the group, but wrote that age prevented. Then, unexpectedly in the same year, the government, for whom he did work with the Assay Office, sent him on a mission to California. He routed his return trip by Denver and made the trip to Georgetown in late September. With his daughter and friends he arranged for horses to take them up the mountain. They were warned that the weather was unpredictable, but the elderly doctor had his heart set on reaching the top of "his" mountain.

The weather turned cold as the horses plodded up the trails, and at twelve thousand feet, a sharp wind began to blow. Reluctantly Torrey realized that the altitude was taxing his heart and lungs, with the hardest part still ahead. He looked wistfully at the towering mass of the twin peaks, Gray and Torrey, then dismounted and took shelter in a lonely log cabin. While the others went on, he built a fire in the stove. As the wind howled and the snow began to fly, he looked around for

supplies. When the others returned after a successful but arduous trip, he was waiting with a hot
lunch for them.

It must have been a sad time of reflection for Dr.
Torrey, staying behind in the rough cabin. He knew
then that he would never climb his mountain—but
instead of dwelling on his misfortune, he thought
ahead to the more pressing needs of his compan-
ions.

Perhaps this is a clue to meeting disappointment.
Accept failure realistically in reaching for goals
beyond your powers. Put aside resentment and
frustration to turn your hand to helping someone
else.

*May we accept our limitations without bitterness
and, without brooding, turn our thoughts to others.*

sensitive plants

But the wisdom that is from above is first pure, then peaceable, gentle, and easy to be entreated, full of mercy and good fruits.

James 3:17

My friends, who are fascinated with the tiny flowers of the tundra, were delighted one day to find a patch of little blue moss gentians. They set about photographing the tiny blooms, lying prostrate to focus their cameras. When they were ready, they were surprised to find that the flowers had closed—for this was a sensitive plant and the shadows cast in setting up the cameras had cut off essential light. After a long interval of waiting, they saw the petals open again and took their pictures—with due respect.

Sensitive children are like this. A threatening shadow, and they close up, retreating within themselves. Parents know what deep-rooted effects teachers can have. A teacher to whom a child feels antagonistic can damage both his confidence and his desire to do well. On the other hand, a teacher whose personality is sunny and warm can make school a joy and inspire the child to do his best. However, teachers are human too, and not all are endowed with winsome personalities. One experienced mother who had endured cycles of good and bad years gave her youngest some down-to-earth advice about dealing with an unsympathetic teacher. ''You might as well face it,'' she said, ''this won't be one of your happiest years. But when you grow up, you'll have to deal with lots of difficult people; so just accept this, and do the best you can.''

''Don't be so sensitive,'' we're told, or tell ourselves. Easier said than done, we know; but it is sound advice. For people, unlike the moss gentian, can learn to withstand loss of sunshine. The flower is programmed to close up and retreat when its light source is cut off. This may be our instinct; but if we only try, we can withstand hostility, feel compassion for difficult personalities, look objectively at uncongenial situations, and go on undismayed.

Nevertheless, in dealing with persons—child or adult—who we know are easily hurt, let us be careful not to cast shadows.

Help us to look for the truth in criticism that hurts, but to speak gently to those of vulnerable spirit.

water

Thy gardens and thy gallant walks
Continually are green
There grow such sweet and pleasant flowers
As nowhere else are seen.
Quiet through the streets, with silver sound
The flood of life doth flow;
Upon whose banks on every side
The wood of life doth grow.

"F. B. P.," 16th century

"Water is the music of the Alhambra," wrote an Arab poet; and anyone who visits these gardens built by the Moors in Spain six hundred years ago knows exactly what the poet means. There are flowers everywhere in the courts of the fortified palace and the summer palace on the hill, but one remembers best the enchantment of the water. The Moors revived techniques of irrigation forgotten since Roman times, and carried water from a river up to the crest of the foothills of the Sierra Nevada, from where it flowed down through many waterways. There are fountains, reflecting pools, waterfalls, and even a hollowed out balustrade filled with rushing water. There is no more refreshing sound in a hot country than the splash and gentle trickling of fountains.

These gardens, and those of the Taj Mahal, are only two of many beautiful Moslem creations. Heaven, to the Moslem, was a garden and, as described in the Koran, a garden not very different from those on earth—except for the beautiful maids and young men who would never grow old.

There is a river, too, in the vision of heaven described in the book of Revelation. But though it waters the tree of life and its fruits, it flows less through a garden than a place of splendor, with its gold, jasper, emerald, and amethyst.

Some of us, who are less visionary, can recall mountain spots that seemed close to paradise. I remember particularly, a little stream tumbling over rocks making tiny pools high on a mountain slope. The banks were edged with moss, mint, and wild strawberries—on either side the tall lodgepole forest. There was wind in the pines and the chatter of squirrels; but loveliest of all was the music of the splashing, tumbling, crystal-clear water.

We have always known that in arid countries water is precious, but many of us grew up thinking that water was something we just had, like air. We know better now, both in cities battling pollution and in the Southwest, where sun seekers are flocking to build. Increasingly, we understand the symbolism of the precious water—of springs in dry valleys, water in the wilderness, and the living water, the cup of cold water. Without pure water we cannot live. It is precious, both as symbol and reality.

We thank thee for the lovely streams that have made our valleys green, and for the teachings of Christ, which refresh our souls.

two sides
of the fence

Now 'tis the spring, and weeds are shallow-rooted;
Suffer them now, and they'll o'ergrow the garden.
William Shakespeare

"Weeding is no chore for me," a friend explained. "I have a long border along the fence and my neighbor has one on her side, so we get out there and work together, she on her side, I on mine. It's really fun that way."

Gardening, for all its joys, is not usually a sociable occupation. One spades, tills, rakes, and plants, and generally works alone. And yet, it is not lonely. The robins fishing for worms in fresh soil, chickadees chirping overhead, the smell of growing things, and the warmth of the sun and the wind brushing our faces combine to create a sense of belonging to the earth and of relating to the power that brings food and flowers from the seeds we plant.

Nevertheless, as in any other field of art or activity, it is a joy to find another who shares our enthusiasm. An artist or writer works alone. Only another in the same field can appreciate his or her problems, inspirations, and achievements. We enjoy finding fellow garden enthusiasts, and so strong is this bond that we see dozens of associations banding together to specialize in one flower—rose, iris, African violet, Hemerocallis, and others.

Gardening is a love that can cross many lines and gather together people of diverse backgrounds. I like to think of those two neighboring women, whose lives are quite different, whose paths seldom cross otherwise, each beautifying her side of the fence. Fences have their uses. They mark boundaries, keep children in and other people's dogs out. It is a happy situation when neighbors can work together, each on their own side, to keep their gardens weeded and enjoy each other's flowers.

Help us, we pray, to find joy in working with others—whether in our gardens, offices, organizations, or churches—for the common good.

Pincushion

sympathy

To feed some hungry soul each day
With sympathy's sustaining bread.
Louisa May Alcott

The housemother of a college residence came down to breakfast one morning and looked around in dismay. "*Where* are my plants?" she exclaimed. The rooms were bare of the thirty or more pots of flowers and foliage she had tended for several years—all gone except one spindly shoot from a grapefruit seed. It was a traumatic moment for the widow who loved growing things—including students—but if *she* was hurt, the young people were indignant. They had watched with interest the growth of the plants and had often commented on the homey atmosphere they gave the dining and social rooms. *Who would do such a thing?* they wondered. Only another person who had nursed seedlings into flowers could know how the woman felt.

A brief item about the theft appeared in the local paper, and the housemother was amazed at the number of people who understood her loss. The first caller was a child who appeared at the door to give her a little begonia. "I'm sorry you lost your plants," she said. Then came three little sisters with their favorite cactus. "We call it Prickles," the spokesman explained, "but you can name it whatever you like." Local florists sent gift coupons. A mother came with a special plant that had been given to her when a daughter died. Old friends, past and present students, even strangers brought in replacements. Today the public rooms look like a conservatory, with hanging baskets, "friendship plants," bright green shamrocks, Christmas cactus, cyclamen, and ivies in abundance. More than seventy-five gifts, along with dozens of notes and telephone calls, were offered to ease the hurt.

When the woman thinks, sometimes, of the begonia she started from a leaf, that after six years was cascading from a large jardiniere, it is still hard for her to believe that someone would steal it, probably to sell for a profit. But, if the experience revealed callousness, it also revealed caring. There were so many people who could put themselves in her place and feel with her.

In greater losses, such as a child or a wife or a

husband, those who have experienced grief can understand most fully. Those who have met with tragedy, illness, or failure know what suffering is.

Sometimes a loss is irreparable, but sorrow is softened when understanding floods the life of the one bereft. How comforting to be able to say, "I never knew so many people cared."

As Jesus taught compassion, so may we learn to share the sorrows and disappointments of those around us.

a flower
for every citizen

Our England is a garden, and such gardens are not made
By singing:—"Oh how beautiful!" and sitting in the shade.
Rudyard Kipling

Like many western cities, ours, to eastern eyes, might look raw and unfinished. The miners and prospectors, our first settlers, were too busy wresting gold and silver from the mountains to worry about aesthetics. While our main streets are no longer filled with mud or dust, they lack old world elegance. Our trees are sparse, and our parks have been rather bare.

It came as a surprise, therefore, a few years ago, when flower beds began to give color to our parks, municipal grounds, and even to the highway medians. Massive plantings of bulbs, marigolds, dahlias, zinnias, geraniums, petunias, ageratum, and chrysanthemums, all short-stemmed to resist the winds, made the city bright as a garden party. The residents were delighted, and park employees received a stream of comments and compliments from tourists, even truck drivers. One burly fellow called from his cab, "I've been watching those flowers. They sure look nice. Funny, but I get the biggest kick out of them!"

The change may be traced to the parks superintendent, a hardworking, enthusiastic young man who is a firm believer in flowers. He was impressed, during a tour of Europe, with the way homes and public places were adorned with gardens, planters, and flower boxes. He believes in the value of flowers first because they give color and character to public areas and second because they indicate pride on the part of the citizens. When he came to our city, he drew up a ten-year plan for setting out thousands of bulbs and plants, with a goal of having "at least one flower for every citizen." We are well on our way! He hoped, too, that by demonstrating what would grow well and in what setting, residents might find hints for beautifying their own yards.

Flowers are not essential to a well-run community any more than a fine organ is essential to a well-run church, but both show pride and concern. In different ways they are symbols of caring. The heart of Christianity is caring, and it is manifested in many ways. Each of us is in a unique position to use his talents or influence to enhance life for those around him.

Help us, we pray, to set goals that will contribute in some small way to the betterment of our communities and the world beyond.

survival

Little flower—but *if* I could understand
What you are, root and all, and all in all,
I should know what God and Man is.
Alfred, Lord Tennyson

Above timberline is a harsh and windswept land where snow falls early and lies late. The cold in winter is intense and the wind bitter; yet for a few weeks in summer the slopes are clothed in a blanket of tiny flowers. Some look familiar, like the forget-me-not, phlox, and columbine, but they are miniatures of our garden varieties. The ways by which the alpine flowers adapt to their climate are many and marvelous.

These beleaguered wildflowers keep a low profile, hugging the earth to withstand the drying gales. One favorite, old-man-of-the-mountain, resembles a little sunflower, with showy yellow head on a stem of a few inches. The dainty pink moss campion, anchored by a taproot, has a matted cushion that slows evaporation and traps flying bits of leaf and dirt to help build soil. The spring beauty, surrounded with a cluster of succulent leaves, has a taproot that may be more than six feet long. There are other kinds of roots. Mat plants, such as the dwarf clover, send out tough little branches that root where they touch the ground—and hold on for dear life. The exquisite litle Rocky Mountain columbine finds moist pockets of soil in the shelter of boulders.

Growth is slow in high places, in spite of the sunshine, because the weeks are so few from frost to frost. Some plants take years to prepare for blooming. When seasons are too short or conditions adverse, the mature plant does not bloom; but extra strength goes into the roots.

When adverse winds blow across our lives, or our nation's, we might reflect on the ways of the alpine flowers. Faith and conviction can be the taproots that give people strength. Conservation of resources means adapting to conditions and preparing for the future. When the season is not right for action, we must not despair, but be patient.

As man's scientific knowledge grows, may we never lose our humility in contemplating the survival of an alpine flower.

volunteers

As for him who voluntarily performeth a good work, verily God is grateful and knowing.

The Koran

In the foothills, where rains are sparse and native trees few, my husband delights in experimenting with unusual plant species that he feels might grow well on our rocky slopes. One day, when he was clearing brush to set out some bare rootstock, he noticed a whiplike cane about two feet tall. "It's only a volunteer," he reflected, "a little locust. But if it can do that well by itself, I'd better leave it awhile." Today, in spite of its old-fashioned thorns, it is one of our most flourishing trees, with flower clusters in spring and lacy shade all summer.

"Volunteers" come up in odd places. From our carefully tended golden rain tree, a healthy descendant appeared some distance away beside the trash can. From a towering black walnut, with roots nourished by irrigation waters, young hopefuls are evident for a block around. Almost too

71

eager are the little ashes and white poplars that sprout in our hard-won lawn.

Flowers can be volunteers too, as any gardener knows who has found a sunflower among his lilies. How do these surprises come to be? The answer is not hard to find; for the wind, the squirrels, and the birds have ways of distributing seeds, some of which come to earth in good soil.

It would be interesting to know who first used the word "volunteer" for a plant that springs up unbidden from fallen seed. It turns our thought to the human volunteer who, according to the dictionary, "enters some service of [his] own free will." It is fortunate for our communities that there are people who give time of their own free will to lead Scout troops, work in hospitals, teach Sunday school classes, work on Community Funds, serve without pay at sometimes grueling tasks as members of school and town boards. Why do they do these things? Perhaps the answer is not entirely different from that given for the plants growing where one seed has fallen. We may venture to assume that somewhere deep in the mind or subconscious a mysterious seed has fallen on good ground and is blossoming into life. Perhaps parents have set an example of selfless giving. Or perhaps religious conviction or a revered leader has been the inspiration. Many of those we admire as heroes or saints were, in fact, volunteers, because their actions went far beyond duty, activated by some deep force they would not deny.

Where there is good seed fallen on good ground, there is good fruit.

We thank thee for the spontaneity of the volunteer—the unexpected plant and the willing human being. Grant that some unknown potential may flower in our own lives.

Shasta
Daisy

simple memorials

Father, in Thy gracious keeping
Leave we now Thy servant sleeping.
John Ellerton

They loved their gardens, their church, and their mountain cabin in the quiet of the pines. For more than fifty years they had lived, gardened, and taught in our town. He was a professor who had quickened the interest of generations of students in the study of birds and natural science. She was a rock-garden expert whose displays drew many visitors each spring. Always generous with time and knowledge, she spoke to garden clubs, assisted less experienced gardeners, and helped solve problems in a way that made her enthusiasm contagious. When the two perished together in a plane accident, the town was stunned. Then came the question of how to honor their memory.

One thing was certain. They would not have liked a flood of floral pieces, sure to inundate the church when the service was announced. Their friends conferred and sent a notice to the local newspaper asking anyone who wished, to bring garden or wild flowers to the church at the time of the memorial.

The altar table was covered with green branches, brightened with native berries. The chancel steps were banked with evergreens. As friends entered the church to pay final tribute, they walked up the aisle, set small containers of golden banner, harebells, daisies, and penstemons among the greens, or tucked in loose handfuls of zinnias and forget-me-nots.

As the simple service proceeded, the congregation was presented with a display of flowers as simple and casual as one might find on the mountain slopes the couple loved, and where their ashes would soon be scattered.

As I sat there, I thought of another simple memorial for a friend in a country church. Remembering her love for red geraniums, the family suggested that friends bring a pot of these for the chancel. Massed around the altar these bright, homey flowers spoke of her own bright spirit.

A memorial service, when it is right, seems to round out and celebrate a life. In spite of grief, it comes as the resolving chord of a song. When we left the church with its bank of mountain flowers, we knew a sense of fulfillment.

Simplicity has its own eloquence.

In honoring those who have gone, may we, in all simplicity, thank thee for lives that have enriched so many others.

the "misterie of gardening"

All these rely upon their hands, and each is skilful in his own work. Without them a city cannot be established. . . . They keep stable the fabric of the world, and their prayer is in the practice of their trade.
Ecclesiasticus 38:31-32a, 34 RSV

Long before there were labor unions there were guilds of craftsmen who joined forces to protect their standards and their own welfare. One of these was a band of gardeners who came together at least six hundred years ago in the City of London. In 1605 they were granted a charter by James I and became officially "The Worshipful Company of Gardeners." Their motto was, "In the sweat of thy brows shalt thou eat thy bread," certainly true in those ill-paid days. Members were allowed a livery, or distinctive costume, for use on special occasions. They were expected to be regular in church attendance, to help their needy, to provide decent burial, and generally to control "the trade, crafte or misterie of gardening."

No longer do they maintain a market garden in the City with fifteen hundred employees and four hundred apprentices; for there is no commercial gardening in the heart of London. But they still have an office and a library. They present bouquets to royal brides, and participate in efforts to encourage church and public gardens that will beautify the city.

"Misterie" is an archaic word relating to an occupational skill, but sometimes an archaic meaning enriches the modern. There is a mystery connected with every skill. Because I am neither artist nor musician, I marvel at the ability of one who can take a pencil and create a likeness or of a conductor who can lead an orchestra through a symphony without a score. There is little mystery in the unskilled toil of the laborer who tills the soil "by the sweat of his brow" simply to eat. But there are others who seem to be born with a gift for gardening. It is revealed in their patience, their tenderness in handling delicate seedlings, their eagerness to learn, and their intuition about the needs of their plantings. Anyone can go through the mechanical motions, but it is the extra caring and response that make the difference.

The wonder is there for each new generation: the

little boy with his first crop of radishes, his father with a stand of sweet corn, his mother with a rainbow of sweet peas, and the neighbor with his prize roses. Those with a gift for working with the earth know well the ''misterie'' of this most ancient calling.

May we honor the mystery of increase given by thee in our gardens and in our spirits.

ꜰoreꞅunnerꞅ

A professor can never better distinguish himself in his work than by encouraging a clever pupil, for the true discoverers are among them, as comets amongst stars.

Carl Linnaeus

When one travels the sparkling waters of Glacier Bay in Alaska, it is hard to realize that less than two hundred years ago, when Captain George Vancouver was exploring the wilderness, the long bay was still a mass of glacial ice. Then came a warming trend, and the ice receded, leaving a body of water extending more than sixty-five miles to the foot of Muir Glacier. A day's excursion by boat between the snow-capped cliffs, with glimpses of spouting killer whales and seals riding the floating chunks of ice, makes a person feel that he is in a new and young world.

Impressive, too, is the evidence of plant succession so clearly visible along the shore at Bartlett Cove. Here rangers conduct nature walks, explaining the drama of plant life that follows the retreat of the glacier. First come the mosses and lichens on the rocks, then dense mats of dryas on sand and gravel to build soil for the willow, alder, and cottonwood thickets. These are gradually crowded out by spruce, and the spruce, in turn, give way to the climax forests of hemlock. All of these stages may be seen at different sites along the water. As the hemlock becomes king, in the the damp places other growth yields to a vivid green moss.

Just as the nurse trees in our more familiar forests shelter stronger seedlings that will ultimately replace them, the forerunners suffer apparent defeat while making possible the onward march.

Many forerunners in human society are not destined to know fame or success; but consider for a moment their accomplishments. Immigrants toiled in order to give their children education and opportunity; homesteaders broke the soil, experiencing brutal hardship, for the benefit of their children and grandchildren; blacks have risked their lives to break down barriers for others of their race; medical researchers have died in their quest for better drugs or therapy; and the tragic deaths of "freedom fighters" are all too familiar in today's world. Perhaps the most famous forerunner of all was John the Baptist, who proclaimed the message, "Prepare ye the way of the Lord."

In the world of science, advancement often comes through one person's building on the work of another. When we go as far as we can in our own calling, and the result is not what we had hoped for, perhaps we will have marked a trail that another may follow—and go beyond.

As the humble mosses and lichens contribute to the ultimate towering forest, so may our lives, in some small way, contribute to a just and peaceful world.

legacies of love

Yea, I have a goodly heritage.

Psalm 16:6

For forty years they had shared in building a beautiful garden around their home, collecting rare plants, starting perennials from seed and roses from cuttings, and nurturing gifts from other gardens. Finally the time came when they could no longer manage their large property and, with regret, decided to move to an apartment. The purchaser of their home, who was not a gardener, suggested they dispose of their plants as they wished. After the rare specimens went to the city parks, they invited friends and neighbors to take what they liked. And so it came to be that in a score of other gardens, roses, iris, lilies, primrose, and peonies flower year after year, reminding their new owners of generous friends.

We can all think back to friends who have given us things we cherish: a necklace, an antique chest, a picture, a tool, a special book, or an Indian artifact. We have received less tangible gifts as well. There was the friend who listened to our youthful problems and helped, the teacher who opened the door to a lasting interest, parents who believed in us and saw more potential than we did ourselves, the companion who taught us to share delight in the little joys of life, the nature lover who introduced us to the challenge of mountain trails, the friend who showed how to meet tragedy with gallantry, the spiritual leader who inspired our faith, the man or woman who showed us the depth and glory of love. While these persons gave us no flowers to plant in our gardens with spade and trowel, their gifts will continue to bloom in our lives long after their first offering. Part of what we are is due to them.

"Rosemary is for remembrance," said Shakespeare; but other flowers are too, when they come from the garden of a friend.

We thank thee for the gifts from others that have enriched our lives, and pray that something of our own will bloom in another's garden.

flowers for "neighboring"

They helped every one his neighbor; and every one said to his brother, Be of good courage.

Isaiah 41:16

All along his fence were dahlias as tall as a man, a sight that delighted passersby from midsummer to the first frost. Dahlia displays do not appear by themselves each summer in the fashion of day lilies or delphinium. The big dahlias require both work and skill. Their grower, a war veteran with vision so impaired as to preclude many other activities, told me how he dug the roots, stored them at just the right temperature during the winter in an old cistern, started them in a cold frame, and then when the earth was warm enough, moved them to their flowering location. The tuberous roots had to be divided carefully for the next year's bloom, and he always set some aside for "neighboring." When I asked what he meant by that odd expression, he explained, "Oh, I just call it that. I mean the ones I put aside to give to other gardeners and neighbors."

Dahlias

This reminded me of another gardener who practices "neighboring." He is an elderly gentleman with a fine display of flowers around his house, who also sets out iris, "basket of gold," and bachelor's buttons along the back alley to make it pleasing for those who go by there.

There are many ways of neighboring, not only for gardeners, but for others who never touch a trowel. We find it wherever a person is giving his time and using his talent freely for others: the professional singer who volunteers to sing in the choir, the writer who does publicity for community organizations, the lawyer who gives free legal aid, the man who finds time to deliver "Meals on Wheels" once a week, the good cook who takes food to a home where there is illness, the compassionate soul who takes time to visit in nursing homes. Many people with special abilities enjoy sharing—such as one stalwart gardener I know who delights in coming to church on a summer Sunday with a large sack under his arm, after the service distributing golden squash to anyone who can use it.

Paul declares that we have "gifts differing according to the grace that is given us." Let's remember always to set something aside for neighboring.

Open our eyes, we pray, to find opportunities wherein our special gifts or training may be helpful to others.

"bag of possibles"

New time, new favor, and new joys
Do a new song require.

John Mason

Sometimes a career can take a sharp and surprising turn. This happened to a man who had been working in a government office job. A friend gave him a handful of blue spruce seeds and suggested he plant them in his garden. The little trees came up, were transplanted, and—in the meantime—sparked such an interest in native plants that eventually this man established a nursery specializing in stock from the wild.

In the fall he roamed the mountains, listening for the special chatter of squirrels that have a seed cache nearby. When he saw a circle of dried cone scales at the foot of the tree, he knew he would find a hoard with seeds for as many as eight species of conifers. He never took them all, but he helped himself with a clear conscience, knowing that squirrels hide away much more than they can use. He gathered seed from the shimmering aspens, which are hard to transplant, and found eager customers for his saplings both here and abroad. He searched, too, for plants thriving under harsh conditions that might adapt well for home landscaping. Such varieties as mountain mahogany, cliffrose, pussytoes, rabbit brush, sage, thimbleberry, and yuccas.

Much in demand as a speaker for garden groups, our friend arrives with what he calls his "bag of possibles." He explains that the old miners wore a leather bag around their necks with such handy items as tobacco, string, knives, matches, and medicines. *His* bag of possibles includes specimens of unusual, native items he has raised for home cultivation.

"Our area is full of newcomers from other parts of the country," he reports. "They all want to plant the things they enjoyed 'back home'—dogwood, rhododendrons, beeches, and tulip trees. I tell them that on old maps this part of the country was marked 'Great American Desert,'" and it's just too dry and arid for their old favorites. What our newcomers have to learn is that we have many plants and trees that *will* grow. They're different, yes, but they have their own beauty."

In our own lives we may face changed conditions. We move as strangers to a new community.

We change jobs. Poor health or budget retrench-
ment require different life-styles. Now is not the
time to brood on what we have left behind but to
adapt to new conditions. Now is the time to explore
our own bag of possibles!

*When the circumstances of our lives change,
help us, while grateful for the good things we have
known in the past, to be open to the new. May we
always look forward, confident, through faith, of
thy guidance.*

a bouquet for the bride

Every good gift and every perfect gift is from above,
and cometh down from the Father of lights.

James 1:17

A friend whose husband was a clergyman told
me about her experiences during World War II,
when her husband's pastorate was in a small town
near an army base.

"Many couples came to our house to be married
by my husband. Our hearts went out to them. They
were so young, and their future was such a question
mark! Usually there was no time for their families
to come and join them, no bridesmaids with pretty
dresses, not even a special gown for the bride. All
they knew was that they wouldn't have much time
together for a long time—if ever. We always tried
to make something special of the occasion: candles,
a nice table, and, when we could, simple refresh-
ments. My husband loved gardening, and one thing
he always did in summer was to go out and pick a
bouquet of flowers. 'A bride should always have
flowers,' he would say.

"I can't tell you how many letters came back thanking us for making the wedding memorable. And most of all they thanked him for the bride's bouquet."

How much a simple gesture can mean! Here was something that cost nothing, but that spoke to the heart, that would be long remembered.

Some people have the gift of knowing how to make a gesture meaningful or a few words memorable. This intuition is shown in many ways: the adult who sits down on the floor to talk with a child, the friend who sends just the right book to one in trouble, the person who reaches out to a stranger and makes him feel welcome, or the one who can say to a loser, "You tried, you did well. I know you will try again." Those of us who were not born with the right words on the tips of our tongues still may grow in thoughtfulness. It helps to think of the things that are most important in another's life and to reach out to those concerns.

The flowers for the bride said without words, "We know what this day means in your life. We know you wish it might be different, but the flowers are a symbol of the joy we hope you will have—we care."

The perfect gift is the one that shows another understands.

Help us to be sensitive to the hungers of others and to perceive thirst that we can quench with that perfect gift, the cup of cold water given in thy name.

is our gardening ever done?

Though I am an old man, I am a young gardener.

Thomas Jefferson

There comes a moment toward the end of the summer when one looks at the garden a bit wearily and thinks, "This is it! No matter what I do now, this is the best it will be." Some of the brightest flowers have gone to seed. Many young plants will not mature before frost. One can always weed, but soon winter will kill the weeds. The temptation is to say "Why bother?" and to toss off the garden gloves and hang up the spade.

As the years pass, we can experience a similar feeling that may come in devastating flashes. "This is it! This is my life. I'm never going to be young and eager again. I'll never be richer or better looking or a spectacular success. This is all there's going to be—so why bother?"

We all know people who, so to speak, have hung up the spade and are interested only in enjoying themselves. They lose themselves in TV, enter into a restless social round, and shy away from responsibility in church and community because they have "done their work."

But not all gardeners give up at summer's end. The expert looks ahead, divides clumps of perennials, makes notes on what has done well, plans changes in planting and color effects, decides what to drop and what to add. As he puts in bulbs for spring blooming, he enjoys the visions of a better garden.

In the same way, there are thoughtful—and often happier—people who ask, "What can I do now that will count later?" Often the answer is found in identifying themselves with a concern wider and farther reaching than their own personal lives. It may be the church, the United Nations, groups working for better government, or compassionate care for those in distress. Involvement may take the form of financial support, letters to the editor, volunteering for whatever jobs one can do, encouraging others, drawing in new people, becoming informed through reading, and praying for God's guidance. It is always possible to identify oneself with some work that casts a longer shadow than one's personal life.

Instead of saying "What's the use?" we can,

like the good gardener, ask, "What can I do now to make this place more beautiful in time to come?"

May we learn from past experience, use our talents, and always look forward to a finer flowering in thy honor.

ꝺʀieꝺ materials

I love to see, when leaves depart,
The clear anatomy arrive,
Winter, the paragon of art,
That kills all forms of life and feeling
Save what is pure and will survive.

Roy Campbell

The rancher on the western plains must consider
it fantastic that city dwellers would pay good
money for stalks of dried yucca, curly dock, or
honey locust pods. Yet, at the November sale held
at the Denver Botanic Gardens, the "Dried
Materials" section is always crowded, resulting in
the gathering of hundreds of dollars toward the
support of the Gardens. Although the price for such
things as acorns, horse chestnuts, cones, and
sweet-gum balls can be as low as a penny, they are
sold quickly, probably to reappear in Christmas
decorations. The more expensive items, such as
teasels, branches of corkscrew willow, bittersweet,
dried Bells of Ireland, and "money plant" vanish
as well.

In earlier days, when winter killed the flowers,

there was not much to brighten our ancestral parlors except "everlastings" and sprays of crimson bittersweet. Today, when fresh flowers are available all year at the florists, and often in the supermarkets, it is surprising how much appeal the dried materials hold. They hold their own, too, against the flood of uncannily "real" plastic flora.

Perhaps part of the appeal of the dried items comes from nostalgia for country living. With their warm, mellow brown colors, they are souvenirs of the outdoors for many city dwellers, stirring up happy associations with summers in the country or holidays on family farms.

Another reason for their appeal might be a new appreciation for the beauty of form. Stark simplicity goes well with modern interiors. A blooming yucca is a handsome sort of candle, with waxy blossoms above pointed leaves on a stiff stalk. When summer ends, the stalks still hold empty brown pods, and their bell-shaped outline is a joy. The oriental poppy in bloom is a handsome flower, but, when the bright petals fall and the stems dry, the intricate structure of the seedpods makes them collectors' items. Here in our dried plants, fruits, and pods, we can look, undistracted by color or setting, at marvels of design.

Even so, undistracted by superficial attractions, we sometimes perceive human character in all its strengths and wonderful complexity.

We thank thee for the diversity of design that we find in snowflakes, plants, and human character. Make us sensitive to its wonder and to thy divine purpose.

secret gardens

Harms of the world have come unto us,
Cups of sorrow we yet shall drain;
But we have a secret that doth show us
Wonderful rainbows in the rain.

Richard Realf

When I was a child, I loved reading *The Secret Garden* by Frances Hodgson Burnett, the story of a lonely child who found the key to a beautiful, mysterious garden, where she found happiness.

There is great charm in the thought of a secluded garden where clematis clothes the walls and a little fountain plays among beds of roses and forget-me-nots. The crusaders brought back from the East the idea of the walled pleasure garden where one could find privacy and could enjoy, in safety, a respite from the rough, noisy life of medieval castles. We see quaint representations of these gardens in old prints and in the stylized designs of oriental rugs.

The cloisters of early monasteries were built around an inner court where, safe from roaming animals, marauders, and worldly distractions, the monks could refresh their spirits in the sunlight as they paced the stone walks with their breviaries. There were gardens in these courts where greens were raised for the table, herbs for seasoning and medicine. Indeed, much of what we know of botany and the apothecary's skill was preserved in the cloisters by the monks of the Dark Ages.

Perhaps we all need secret gardens to refresh our spirits. They might take many forms in addition to the modern secluded patio or the backyard plot where one may catch the fragrance of sun-ripened tomatoes, strawberries, and petunias. Secret gardens might be a carpenter's workshop, a painter's studio, an apartment dweller's collection of house plants, a child's tree house or playhouse, a scholar's library, a photographer's darkroom, or a wooded trail. There are many ways in which people may turn from daily routine for renewal.

There are gardens of spiritual refreshment as well. Some are found through reading books of inspiration or studying sacred writings. Some are found in quiet moments of meditation and prayer. Often they are found in worship at a beloved church. Coming together with a congregation may not seem to be entering a secret garden, but each person's heart is secret; and the inspiration that comes to it through worship is known to him alone.

Grant that each of us may seek sources of refreshment that will lead to more inspired and effective living.

Rediscovery

For there is hope of a tree, if it be cut down, that it will sprout again. . . . Though the root thereof wax old in the earth, and the stock thereof die in the ground; yet through the scent of water it will bud, and bring forth boughs like a plant.

Job 14:7-9

When the couple bought their property from a subdivided ranch, they were delighted to have some big cottonwoods and a few willows along a ditch, but the rest of the ground was so sunbaked with tangled dry grass that they wondered if anything would ever grow around the home they planned to build. Nevertheless, they set out some flowering shrubs and began to water. The next spring their bushes leafed out in healthy fashion; and, as the season progressed, they found some unsuspected bonuses. Old roses they had not even noticed, suddenly appeared, developing fat buds. Cultivated monarda, different from the mountain native, began to add a splash of crimson; and even some lilies ventured out of hiding, lured by the "scent" of water. There was no question now that their home could be set amidst a garden.

People can be like dry land. They may seem closed up, repressed, withdrawn into themselves, until a friendly interest makes possible the flowering of hidden capabilities.

This can be true not only of individuals but of groups. A minister comes to a static church and through purpose and love of people creates a new atmosphere. A skillful and enthusiastic photographer joins a dying camera club, and within a short time new talent is attracted, and the whole standard of excellence goes up. A perceptive teacher takes a problem class and, through understanding, kindles in the pupils a desire to achieve. In all of these situations, talents and aspirations were lying dormant. The men Jesus chose as his disciples were neither impressive nor inspiring until his faith in them brought forth their latent and unsuspected powers.

Job laments that, unlike the dry tree that will sprout again when refreshed by water, man goes down to dust. What he does not say, however, is that man, discouraged and oppressed, can, with the healing magic of encouragement, flower into unimagined fulfillment during his allotted span of years.

As we water dry ground to make it flower, so may we, through encouragement and understanding, help others to realize their potential.

"god wot"

A garden is a lovesome thing, God wot!
  Rose plot,
  Fringed pool,
Ferned grot—
  The veriest school
  Of Peace; and yet the fool
Contends that God is not—
Not God! in gardens! when the eve is cool?
  Nay, but I have a sign:
  'Tis very sure God walks in mine.

Thomas Edward Brown

Leafing through anthologies of poetry, one finds many fine tributes to flowers and gardens, but all very much alike. They are apt to be variations on four themes: melancholy, reassurance, joy, and inspiration.

Flowers are beautiful, but alas, their time is brief and so is ours. Many poets echo the psalmist, "As for man, his days are as grass: as a flower of the field, so he flourisheth. For the wind passeth over it, and it is gone."

However, some find reassurance in the thought

that flowers die but will bloom again. In Longfellow's words, they are:

> Emblems of our own great resurrection
> Emblems of the bright and better land.

More joyous reflections are Wordsworth's who
finds flowers so lovely they can make the heart
glad, even in memory. Thinking of a host of
daffodils, he finds,

> They flash upon that inward eye
> Which is the bliss of solitude;
> And then my heart with pleasure fills,
> And dances with the daffodils.

How many gardeners, including nonpoets, feel
close to God as they work in their gardens! Perhaps
the most familiar poem expressing this thought was
written a scant century ago by Thomas E. Brown, a
native of the Isle of Man. Brown knew an unhappy
youth as one of the many children of a poverty-
ridden clergyman. He had a brilliant mind, but
when at the age of fifteen he went to King
William's College, he had to go with a
"servitorship"—a scholarship, but one that meant
working as a servant, wearing special clothes, and
eating at a different time from the more fortunate

students. This was a painful experience for the sensitive boy. His later career as a teacher was frustrating and unfulfilling, but he left a brief verse that appears on thousand of plaques and speaks the feelings of millions. While any modern poet suspects the word "wot" is used for rhyming convenience, this does not dim the appeal of his poem.

No doubt poets will continue to write of their sense of a divine presence close to them among the sunlit flowers, but possibly there is not much new to add. Thomas Brown has said it. Truly "a garden is a lovesome thing—God wot."

We thank thee for human longing to make the earth beautiful. May we sense thy presence in the gardens of our lives.